TRACY FOX

Speaker – Author – Life Coach

Other books by Tracy Fox
Available on Amazon.com:

Happy Self–A Three Step Strategy To Elevate Your Inner Game

The Having A Heart For God Devotional

Happy Marriage™ Handbook

For Her

Tracy Fox

Contents

Who I Am And What's Inside

Hi Everyone,

My name is Tracy Fox and I am a speaker, author and certified life coach. I teach actionable strategies so that you can enjoy a Happy Self, a Happy Marriage and a Happy Life. I work with clients all over the country, both in person and on the phone. Over my 10 years of personal coaching, I have spent countless hours listening, brainstorming and consulting with both men and women about how to elicit the best from themselves and their marriages.

In this *Happy Marriage Handbook*, I take the most effective, proven strategies and techniques and put them together in one place to give you a portfolio of answers on how to enjoy a long-lasting, successful union. I have identified 10 key areas where most couples get off track. This workbook will enable you to gain clarity around your marital goals and the exact steps to implement them. There is a Happy Marriage handbook for Her and a Happy Marriage handbook for Him. After you complete your answers, simply spend time together, discussing and collaborating how to design the Happy Marriage of your dreams. I have also developed an on-line course, by the same, Happy Marriage, name. If you want or need an audio/visual component with weekly email reminders to do the 10 lessons, you can subscribe at my website, **www.tracyfox.net**.

I, myself, have been married for over 20 years and I have put all ten solutions listed in this book to the test. The key to a long-term successful marriage is being intentional. My hope is that you will use this manual as a fun, creative undertaking to better yourself, your marriage, your family and your entire life as a whole.

In each section, you are invited to write answers down in the space provided. Statistics prove that people who write things down have a 90% better chance of manifesting their hopes and dreams into a new reality. Enjoy this process and do it with the intention of a Happy Marriage for the rest of your life.

Please reach out to me with any concerns or questions.

Sincerely,

Tracy

Tracy Fox
203 856-2906
www.tracyfox.net

Introduction

Welcome to the *Happy Marriage Handbook*. There is no better investment of time and energy than your personal dedication to creating a Happy Marriage.

Let's Look At Why Happy Marriage Is Good For You And Your Spouse.

1. Married couples do better in <u>EVERY</u> indicator of health and well-being.

2. Married couples enjoy a stronger sense of identity.

3. Married couples have richness of social connectivity and belonging.

4. Married couples have less stress and live longer.

5. In virtually every way that social scientists can measure, married people do better than unmarried or divorced people. They live happier, more intimate and more affluent lives.

A Happy Marriage Is Also GREAT For Your Children. Children From Intact Married Families Are:

1. More likely to attend college

2. Enjoy overall higher levels of happiness

3. Less likely to do drugs

4. Less likely become pregnant in teen years

5. Less likely to be abused

6. Less likely to slip into poverty

7. Less likely to go to jail

8. Less likely to experience divorce themselves

Statistics Prove That Couples Who Do The Work To Create A Happy Marriage, Stay Together Happily Ever After.

It turns out that 90% of couples who hit a very serious trouble spot in their marriage, but stayed and did the work to transform their union, are in fact, completely happy again in their married life up to 10 years later. They also report they are pleased they did not go through with divorce as an option.

The truth is that you can create any marriage you want. So why not create the Happy Marriage of your dreams.

Remember:

Happy Marriage
A 10-Step Solution To Happily Ever After!

Solution #1
Esteem Your Marriage Above All Else

Solution #2
Create A Marital Mission Statement

Solution #3
Commit To A Weekly Meeting

Solution #4
Contribute In Thought, Word and Deed

Solution #5
Master Your Money

Solution #6
Encourage Intimacy, Sex and Celebration

Solution #7
Revere Conflict

Solution #8
Go Team Parent

Solution #9
Forgive, Forget, Get A Fresh Start

Solution #10
Keep The Faith

Solution # 1

Esteem Your Marriage Above All Else

Solution #1 for a Happy Marriage is to esteem your marriage above all else. To esteem means: "To regard highly or favorably; regard with respect or admiration." This is a personal commitment to continually set your marriage apart from the ordinary as you strive for the two of you to become one unit.

If you are like most couples, on your wedding day you enthusiastically commit to the "sanctity" of marriage, all while vowing in front of God, family or friends to deeply care for one another for the rest of your lives. Your ceremony is a public declaration of love and commitment. You repeat and truly mean words similar to the following: "To have and to hold, from this day forward, for better, for worse, for richer, for poorer, in sickness and in health, to love and to cherish, until death do you part."

However, over the years, your marriage may get off track due to daily distractions or busyness. The authentic "loving" and "cherishing" can disappear from your interactions altogether. Little by little, you might move in different directions, away from each other, or you could get lazy about maintaining a stellar union. Circumstances, bickering, daily survival and boredom can steal the joy of marital bliss. You can transform that immediately. It starts with redefining the idea of how you "esteem your marriage."

Let's Be Honest
(Write Your Answers Down In The Space Provided)

Based on the definition of "esteem" above, do you esteem your marriage? YES___NO___

What do you think to yourself about your marriage?

_____

_____

_____

_____

What do you say to your spouse about your marriage?

_____

_____

_____

_____

When you describe married life to friends, what exact words do you use?

_____

_____

_____

_____

Where do you see your marriage in 20 years?

_____

_____

_____

_____

Is your marriage a top priority? YES___NO___

Name two actions that prove you "esteem" your marriage.

1)_____

_____

_____

2)_____

_____

_____

If you asked others, what would they say about your marriage?

_____

_____

_____

_____

What is one new insight you have about your marriage after answering the questions above?

_____

_____

_____

_____

Here Is The THREE-STEP STRATEGY To Esteem Your Marriage

1) You reclaim the original wedding vow as a daily commitment
2) You behave as "two becoming one unit"
3) You remember that how you identify something is how you will treat it

FIRST STRATEGY To Esteem Your Marriage Is To Reclaim Your Marriage Vow Daily

Most of us wrote, recited or repeated wedding vows that resembled the one below.

> I Take Thee...To Be My Spouse....
> to have and to hold from this day forward;
> for better or for worse,
> for richer and for poorer,
> in sickness and in health;
> to love, honor and cherish;
> loving you more tomorrow than I do today;
> until death do us part.

Let's Be Honest
(Write Your Answers Down In The Space Provided)

Do you remember your wedding vow? YES___NO___

What are the top key components of your wedding vow you believed you would always honor?

_____

_____

_____

_____

What does it really mean to love, honor and cherish till death do you part?

_____

_____

_____

_____

Are you doing this in your daily-married life? YES___NO___

What areas of your original wedding vow could you improve on?

_____

_____

_____

_____

What are you willing to do differently toward the goal of having a Happy Marriage?

_____

_____

_____

_____

Can you imagine how different your marriage would be if you lived out your original wedding vow week-in and week-out? YES___NO___

In what three specific ways could your marriage be improved if you followed your vows more closely?

1)_____

_____

2)_____

_____

_____

3)_____

_____

_____

SECOND STRATEGY To Esteem Your Marriage Is To Behave As Two Become One Unit

When you got married, you intentionally committed to two people becoming intertwined as one unit. Marriage creates "one body" as a new reality. It is meant to promote the good of the couple, the family, and the community as a whole.

The word "matrimony" itself is from the Old French word "matremoine," which comes directly from the Latin word "matrimonium" and means "wedlock" or "marriage." It has the idea of being locked together on a permanent basis.

This idea is rooted in the original definition of marriage found in the Old Testament – Genesis 2:24 "*This explains why a man leaves his father and mother and is joined to his wife, and the two are united into one."*

And emphasized by Jesus in the New Testament in Mathew 19:4-6, *"Haven't you read," he replied, "that at the beginning the Creator 'made them male and female,' and said, 'For this reason a man will leave his father and mother and be united to his wife, and the two will become one flesh'? So they are no longer two, but one flesh. Therefore what God has joined together, let no one separate."*

In other words, in marriage, we become one in unity, one in purpose, and one in mind. This "joining" is meant to be so strong that we merge into the same ONE person, that it is like one part of the other will be ripped away from the other if they are ever separated. We are told to cleave and never leave because what God has joined together, no one should try to separate.

Tracy's Tip

I like to illustrate this concept another way. Most people regard their marriage as x/x. They live together, they create a life together, but they are not really completely together. To create a Happy Marriage, you need to leave your side of the line and join your spouse so that you merge into the same person.

In a Happy Marriage 1 plus 1 no longer equals 2.

INSTEAD 1 + 1 = 1.

Circle How You Rate Your Marriage Being "One Unit" In These Areas:

Emotionally?

1   2   3   4   5   6   7   8   9   10

Physically?

1   2   3   4   5   6   7   8   9   10

Mentally?

1   2   3   4   5   6   7   8   9   10

Spiritually?

1   2   3   4   5   6   7   8   9   10

Financially?

1   2   3   4   5   6   7   8   9   10

Based On Your Ratings:
What Areas Do You Need To Improve?

_____

_____

_____

_____

Name 3 Things You Could You Do To Be More Connected In Key Areas Of Marriage?

1) _____

2) _____

3) _____

How Do You Think "Two Become One" Was Meant To Be Experienced In Marriage?

_____

_____

_____

_____

THIRD STRATEGY To Esteem Your Marriage Is To Remember How You Identify Your Marriage is How You Will Treat It

The truth is that how we identify something is in fact how we will treat it. Let me give you an example of the gift of an old book. If someone gives you a dusty, old book and you don't realize its value, then you are likely to put it away, pay no attention to it or simply throw it out with the rest of the trash.

However, when you discover that the same book is a First Edition Hemingway, it is no longer just a dusty old book, it is now invaluable. You proudly place it on the mantel, show it off to friends and family and guard it from any harm.

The same thing is true of a HAPPY MARRIAGE – Identify your marriage as something extremely worthwhile and you will protect it, honor it and cherish it above all else.

Let's Be Honest
(Write Your Answers Down In The Space Provided)

How are you identifying your marriage?
Are you thinking… *"This is a drag"* OR *"I love being married!"*

_____

_____

_____

Do you cherish your spouse in marriage? Are you saying… *"I wish I hadn't married you"* OR *"I am so happy I chose you to be my partner"*?

_____

_____

_____

Are you positively sharing your married life with friends and family?

Are you articulating…*"We never see each other"* OR *"This marriage is the most important thing in my life."*?

_____

_____

_____

In What Specific Four Ways Could You Honor Your Marriage In More Positive Ways?

1)_____

_____

_____

2)_____

_____

_____

3)_____

_____

_____

"Happily ever after is not a fairy tale. It's a choice."

- Fawn Weaver

Lock In the Learning

What is one action you will take to "esteem" your marriage?

_____

_____

_____

_____

NOTES

_____

_____

_____

_____

_____

_____

_____

_____

_____

_____

_____

_____

_____

_____

Remember To   _____

Share Your New   _____

Insights With   _____

Your Spouse   _____

_____

Solution # 2

Create A Marital Mission Statement

Solution #2 for a Happy Marriage is to create a Marital Mission Statement that serves as a declaration of the pre-eminent interests of both spouses. It reflects the combined values, goals and purpose for why your marriage exists. Every successful business has a mission statement because this is how companies stay on the same page with employees and customers as it enable them stay true to their goals and vision for what they want to accomplish.

The same can be true for a Happy Marriage. A marriage is similar to a business whose purpose is the management of a shared life. The Marital Mission Statement helps you get excited about designing and maintaining your own happily ever after.

A Marital Mission Statement serves marriage in the following ways:

1) A good Marital Mission Statement determines the marriage's direction. Smart spouses use the mission statement to remind themselves why they got married and what strategies to employ for their long-term partnership to succeed.

2) A good Marital Mission Statement focuses on the marriage possibilities. It provides a template for decision-making and a road map for goals, values and agendas.

3) A good Marital Mission Statement facilitates evaluation and improvement. It also enables partners to reconsider strengths and weaknesses in communication and then choose other strategies for success.

What it really does is put YOU in control of your own marriage!!!

Before constructing your own Marital Mission Statement...Let's answer some questions that will help you gain clarity on the exact type of union you wish to create.

Let's Be Honest
(Write your answers down in the space provided)

Question #1
Why Did You Get Married In the First Place? What were your original aspirations for your marriage? Was it to be singularly committed to one person, to start a family or to honor a sacred union?

_____

_____

_____

_____

Question #1
What is important for your marriage to succeed? Some Ideas might include: Honesty, Being Debt Free, Humor, Social Connections, Extended Family Involvement, Deepening Your Faith, Spending More Time Together.

_____

_____

_____

_____

Question #3

What Values Do You Want to Promote In Your Marriage? Some Values might include: Fairness, Compassion, Faith, Loyalty, Openness, Pleasure, Responsibility, Service, Wealth, Wisdom, Success, Creativity or Integrity.

_____

_____

_____

_____

Question #4

What Future Goals Do You Want to Achieve in Your Marriage? Some Ideas include: Owning A Home, Starting A Business, Adopting a Child, Traveling the World, Being Mission Oriented, Or Having a Big Family.

_____

_____

_____

_____

Name four words you want to describe your marriage?

1)_____ 2)_____ 3)_____ 4)_____

How do you want your partner to treat you?

_____

_____

_____

_____

How do you want to treat your spouse?

_____

_____

_____

_____

What home environment do you want to create?

_____

_____

_____

_____

What ideals do you want to promote for your marriage?

_____

_____

_____

_____

How do you want others to view your marriage?

_____

_____

_____

_____

What is one aspect of your marriage that must change?

_____

_____

_____

_____

Who is someone you know that has a stellar marriage?

_____

What do you admire about their marriage?

_____

_____

_____

_____

What is one insight you have about a Marital Mission Statement?

_____

_____

_____

_____

Once the questions above are answered, consider what you have written and then co-produce a statement that elicits the best ideas from your Happy Marriage handbook and your spouse's. When you have completed it, place it confidently where it can be viewed and revisited often.

Here Are The Guidelines For Writing Your Marital Mission Statement

1) Keep It Simple
2) Be Authentic
3) Use Proactive Verbs On What You Want To Accomplish
4) Make Sure You Both Agree

5) Keep It Up To Date

6) Place It Where It Can Be Seen by Both Of You Regularly

7) Review Often and Make Adjustments Where Necessary

8) Have Fun While Writing YOUR Marital Mission Statement

9) Remember, You Can Create ANY Marriage You Desire So Be A Possibility Thinker!

Here is a great quote by Dee Hock, Founder of Visa, which articulates why a Mission Statement is good for any organization including A Happy Marriage.

"I believe that purpose and principle clearly understood and articulated, and commonly shared, are the genetic code of any healthy organization. To the degree that you hold purpose and principles in common among you, you can dispense with command and control. People will know how to behave, in accordance with them and they will do them in thousands of unimaginable creative ways. The organization will become a vital, living set of beliefs."

The point of A Marital Mission Statement is to be intentional today so you can have a Happy Marriage tomorrow.

Tracy's Tip

Being intentional in your marriage creates endless possibilities for positive change, because if you know where you are going you are a lot more likely to get there. An intention is a clear and positive statement of an outcome you want to experience. It is a goal, or vision, that guides your activities, thoughts, attitudes, and choices. It requires detailed planning and specific definition of your desired outcome.

A Marital Mission Statement is a lot like a GPS system found in many cars. It shows you the clear path to where you want to go. It knows where you are starting your journey and then once you enter a destination, it calculates a direct path so you don't get off track.

Here are samples Marital Mission Statement:

- "To enjoy a lasting partnership where both people get their needs met and their desires fulfilled."

- "Make our home a place where kindness rules and together we create fun, prosperity and harmony."

- "Always be respectful and full of genuine love for each other as we continually cherish and honor this relationship. Above all else, we check in and contribute daily to keep our marriage happy and in good standing."

- "1. Rise Above the Routines & Pressure of Daily Life.
  2. Show Consistent Support To Each Other.
  3. Encourage and Accept Each Other As We Are.
  4. Be Debt Free.
  5. Have A Home Where Laughter and Faith Are Top Priority."

Write your Marital Mission Statement below.

_____

_____

_____

_____

_____

_____

_____

Compare your Marital Mission Statement with your spouse's and then write one together that will guide your Happy Marriage into Happily Ever After.

"A great marriage is not when the 'perfect couple' comes together. It is when an imperfect couple learns to enjoy their differences."

- Dave Meurer

Lock In the Learning

What is one action you will take for your Marital Mission Statement?

_____

_____

_____

_____

NOTES

_____

_____

_____

_____

_____

_____

_____

_____

_____

_____

Remember To   _____

Share Your New   _____

Insights With   _____

Your Spouse   _____

                              _____

                              _____

Solution # 3

Commit To A Weekly Meeting

Solution #3 for a Happy Marriage is to commit to a Weekly Meeting. A Weekly Meeting keeps you accountable to honing and re-evaluating strategies that work in your union. It enables both partners to discuss pressing matters in a safe, non-critical arena. Here you continue to look at your Marital Mission Statement and address both old and new business as well as future agendas for keeping your marital lives on track. Goal setting and planning are highlighted. An additional benefit to a Weekly Meeting is that you save all the potential "hot spots" for a one-time session. This allows for a conflict free zone the rest of the week.

The Weekly Meeting is a time when you and your spouse meet every week to discuss the operation of your marriage. This will include all the moving pieces that need to be addressed, managed and kept on track. It sounds dry and boring; however, The Weekly Meeting is my #1 secret to a Happy Marriage.

Why? I have highlighted this one strategy in every personal marriage coaching session I do and couples report that results have been life changing and ultimately transformational to their marriage!

Here are the reasons the Weekly Meeting is so crucial to a Happy Marriage:

1. Helps you organize and schedule the week ahead together

2. Removes any surprises or unrealistic expectations of each other

3. Allows you to discuss hot topics in a safe non-critical arena

4. Gives you time to review and discuss what is important to you weekly and then you don't have to keep talking about it all week long.

5. Allows you a moment to see events from the other person's point of view and then brainstorm for a team approach to every issue in your marriage.

Rules For The Weekly Meeting

1. Agree on a time for a One Hour Weekly Meeting.

2. Make this meeting non-negotiable. It must be a top priority as it is critical to your long-term success.

3. Schedule the meeting on both of your calendars.

4. Start with how you want the meeting to end at the beginning of the discussion. Choose to end the meeting as friends, in agreement, in love.

5. Use "I" statements, not "you" statements. This avoids any blame, critical attitudes, or feeling attacked.

6. Don't meet when either of you are hungry, angry or exhausted.

7. Bring an agenda of what you want to discuss.

8. Get rid of the word "compromise" and replace it with the word "negotiate" which empowers each spouse.

Benefits of The Weekly Meeting

- It Builds A Supportive Relationship between You and Your Spouse
- You Will Get Things Done

- You Are Not Bickering at Other Times, as Everything Should be Addressed in The Weekly Meeting

- Issues Get Talked About and Not Swept Under Rug

- It Puts You in Control of Your Marriage

- It Creates A Team Approach To Problem Solving

- It Allows You To ENJOY The Rest Of The Week

Tracy's Tip

Inevitably, clients will tell me:

"this is the greatest idea"

"it totally works"

"whenever we meet the results are amazing"

BUT...

"we didn't meet this week because"

"we are too busy"

"the kids are too busy"

"life is too busy"

Don't make excuses – instead make it happen! Decide that your Weekly Meeting is a non-negotiable and the foundation for your Happy Marriage.

Here are four key areas to discuss weekly:

Finances:
What areas of financial management do you need to discuss every week? Do you need to talk about a budget, monthly bills, cash allowances, or overall planning?

_____

_____

_____

_____

Parenting:
What areas of parenting and family life do you need to discuss every week? Do you need to talk about childcare issues, rules, scheduling, spending more together or family meals?

_____

_____

_____

_____

Romance:
How can you spend more time planning romance and intimate moments together every week? Do you need a date night, a weekend away, more daily affection or general kindness?

_____

_____

_____

_____

The To-Do List:

What tasks need to be put on the "to do" list and who will do them each and every week? Are there bigger projects that need management? How will you delegate?

_____

_____

_____

_____

If you meet consistently and manage the topics that might cause you the most stress, you can avoid trouble spots. Decide to be intentional about having the Happy Marriage of your dreams.

Let's Be Honest
(Write the answers below in the space provided)

Do you think the Weekly Meeting is a good idea? YES____NO____

In what way is the Weekly Meeting a good idea for your marriage?

_____

_____

_____

_____

What do you want to accomplish at the Weekly Meeting?

_____

_____

_____

_____

What is your main goal for the Weekly Meetings?

_____

_____

_____

_____

What other topics need to be discussed at your Weekly Meeting?

_____

_____

_____

_____

How will you show up and how will you treat your spouse during the Weekly Meeting?

_____

_____

_____

_____

How could you use your Marital Mission Statement to re-evaluate your marriage at the Weekly Meeting?

_____

_____

_____

_____

"Many people spend more time in planning the wedding than they do in planning the marriage."

- Zig Ziglar

Lock In the Learning

What is one action you will take regarding a Weekly Meeting?

_____

_____

_____

_____

NOTES

_____

_____

_____

_____

_____

_____

_____

_____

_____

_____

_____

Remember To   _____

Share Your New   _____

Insights With   _____

Your Spouse   _____

_____

_____

Solution # 4

Contribute In Thought, Word And Deed

Solution #4 for a Happy Marriage is to be aware of contributing to your marriage in thought, word and deed. Awareness is what actually changes your marital destiny. You can either be intentional about moving toward your spouse in kindness and connection or away from your spouse in dismissiveness and denial.

Let's think about what the word "contribute" really means. It translates "To give in order to provide something for someone else."

Based on that definition, how do you rate yourself for <u>contribution</u> in your own marriage?

_____

_____

_____

_____

Here are three important ways you can contribute to your Happy Marriage in thought, word and deed:

    1) Say Yes to the Emotional Bid

    2) Know and Meet Your Spouse's Needs

    3) Examine and Use the 5 Love Languages

1) Say Yes to Emotional Bids

John Mordecai Gottman, a professor emeritus in psychology known for his work on marital stability and relationship analysis, made a critical discovery regarding successful marriages. (The following information was taken from his findings) Dr. Gottman invited 130 newlywed couples to spend the day at a retreat and watched them as they did what couples normally do on vacation: cook, clean, listen to music, eat, chat, and hang out. Throughout the day, partners would make requests for connection.

For example, if the husband is a bird enthusiast and he notices a goldfinch fly across the yard, he might say to his wife, "Look at that beautiful bird outside!" He's not just commenting on the bird, he is really requesting a response from his wife, a sign of interest or support.

If the wife turned toward her husband and joined him at the window, she was saying, "yes" to the emotional bid. If the wife turned away, or responded minimally, such as "I am busy, I don't have time to look at the bird now," then she is saying "no" to the emotional bid.

These bidding interactions had profound effects on marital well-being. Couples who had divorced after a six-year follow-up had "turn-toward bids" only 33 percent of the time. Only three in ten of their bids for emotional connection were met with intimacy.

The couples who were still together after six years, had "turn-toward bids" 87 percent of the time. Nine times out of ten, they were meeting their partner's emotional needs.

Let's Be Honest
(Write the answers below in the space provided)

What do you think your emotional bid rate is?_____

What do you think your spouse's emotional bid rate is?_____

Do you express appreciation for your spouse? YES____NO____

What is one thing you could improve in this area?

_____

_____

_____

_____

Do you validate your spouse's feelings even if you disagree? YES____NO____

What is one thing you could improve in this area?

_____

_____

_____

_____

Do you keep up your appearance for your spouse? YES____NO____

What is one thing you could improve in this area?

_____

_____

_____

_____

Do you participate in what your spouse deeply cares about? YES____NO____

What is one thing you could improve in this area?

_____

_____

_____

_____

Do you treat your spouse the same way as when you dated?
YES____NO____

What is one thing you could improve in this area?

_____

_____

_____

_____

How will you make sure that you and your spouse have a high emotional bid rate going forward?

_____

_____

_____

_____

In what specific ways can Dr. Gottman's findings change the way you respond to your spouse?

_____

_____

_____

_____

2) Meet The Needs Of Your Spouse

Spouses have different needs in marriage. It is important to be aware of these so you can meet the needs of the person you love.

Here are the Top Five Marital Needs by spouse:

For Men:	For Women:
1) Sexual Fulfillment	1) Affection
2) Recreational Companionship	2) Conversation
3) Attractive Spouse	3) Honesty & Openness
4) Domestic Support	4) Financial Support
5) Praise and Admiration	5) Family Commitment

Let's Be Honest
(Write the answers below in the space provided)

What would you say are your top needs in marriage?

1. _____

2. _____

3. _____

Does your spouse know and care about your needs? YES____NO____

How would you be willing to express your needs to your spouse?

_____

_____

_____

_____

What would you say are your spouse's top needs in marriage?

1. _____

2. _____

3. _____

Do you know or care about your spouse's top needs? YES___NO____

What is one thing you could do to meet your spouse's needs?

_____

_____

_____

_____

What is one thing your spouse could to do meet your needs?

_____

_____

_____

_____

What will you do to make sure you have ongoing dialog about meeting each other's needs in marriage?

_____

_____

_____

_____

The Five Love Languages: A Brief Synopsis

Dr. Gary Chapman defines five love languages we all use in communicating. He asserts that people communicate and feel love in different ways. Humans all need each of these different things, but typically there is one that really speaks to an individual heart. To really appreciate and understand each other we must consider the love language of our spouse.

The 5 Love Languages are:
Physical Touch - feels love when others touch them lovingly
Acts of Service - feels love when others help them out
Words of Affirmation - feels love when others verbally affirm them
Quality Time - feels love when others spend time with them
Gifts - feels love when others give them thoughtful things

Let's Be Honest
(Write the answers below in the space provided)

What do you normally do to show your spouse you love them?

_____

_____

_____

_____

What is your primary Love Language?

_____

_____

_____

_____

What is your spouse's primary Love Language?

_____

_____

_____

_____

How would it positively alter your relationship if you know and understood each other Love Language? What are you willing to do differently in terms of Love Languages?

_____

_____

_____

_____

Tracy's Tip

The reason the 5 Love Languages make sense is that if a wife's love language is "service," and on an anniversary she tells her husband that all she wants is breakfast in bed, but he doesn't listen to that and instead buys her a new bracelet, then there is going to be a very expensive problem that could have been avoided. The wife will be upset that the husband didn't hear her, and the husband will be hurt that she was not appreciative of all the money and effort he spent on buying a gift. You can avoid all of this by knowing and understanding your spouse's love language.

Being aware that your Love Language is probably different from your spouse's Love Language can help create a Happy Marriage.

"Marriage is not 50-50, Divorce is 50-50. Marriage has to be 100-100. It isn't dividing everything in half, but giving everything you've got!"

- Dave Willis

Lock In the Learning

What is one action you will take to create a spirit of contribution?

_____

_____

_____

_____

NOTES

_____

_____

_____

_____

_____

_____

_____

_____

_____

_____

_____

Remember To   _____

Share Your New   _____

Insights With   _____

Your Spouse   _____

                                         _____

                                         _____

Solution # 5

Master Your Money

Solution #5 for a Happy Marriage is to master your money. Both spouses need to be educated on income, spending, investing and debt so that these concepts emerge as a second language in your discussion of personal finance. This mastery over money will enable you to prosper together.

Several studies over the years indicate that fighting over money is a leading indicator of a future divorce. Research also concludes that arguments about money are longer and usually more intense than other types of marital disagreements. Why? Couples who don't have clarity around their personal finances are doomed to defend their position for control. It's not hard to understand why money can end so many married relationships. Sharing control of your finances with another person means compromise and trust, which can be difficult even with someone you have known for a long time.

Moreover, men and women traditionally view money differently. Women tend to view money as a means of security, while men view it as a source of power and status. The way someone is raised along with their personal history can play a big role in how they deal with money.

In this chapter, you are going to look at different ways to communicate more effectively regarding personal finance. The first thing you must do is meet with your spouse and both of you share the good, the bad and the ugly truth about your finances. Bring credit card statements, pay stubs and copies of credit reports for absolute clarity.

Tracy's Tip

You can get an annual credit report for free! Everybody should know his or her own credit score. www.AnnualCreditReport.com.

Let's Be Honest
(Write the answers below in the space provided)

Have You Started the Conversation?
Do you meet regularly with your spouse to discuss money? Why or why not? How would a financial meeting benefit you?

What will this information tell you?

_____

_____

_____

_____

Where Does the Money Go?
Do you BOTH understand the income and, more importantly, the expenses? What money comes in? What money goes out? In what way do you both understand the personal finances?

_____

_____

_____

_____

Who Pays for What?
Many couples come into a marriage with two very different incomes and two very different ways of dealing with money. What is your system for who pays for what? Do you have one?

_____

_____

_____

_____

Have You Made Long-Term Plans?
Do you have a sound financial plan for paying down debt, an emergency fund, long-term savings funds or college tuition? What have you both done about long-term planning?

_____

_____

_____

_____

Do you BOTH understand the finances?

_____

Who handles the money now?

_____

What financial secrets should you share with your spouse?

_____

_____

_____

_____

Are you taking a team approach to your money?

_____

What is your emergency plan, if someone loses their job?

_____

_____

_____

_____

What specific changes need to be made so you can improve your family finances?

_____

_____

_____

_____

Discuss and Understand These Finance Terms

1. **Earning:** This is an area to discuss whether or not you both plan to have a job, for how long, and how much you each contribute to the marital joint accounts.

2. **Spending:** Here you decide what your priorities are: education, travel, leisure, goods and services, or luxury items.

3. **Accounting:** This is where you decide who will keep track of your overall net worth. Will you have a budget? And how will you divide the financial tasks in your relationship?

4. **Saving:** This is a place to make decisions about what proportion of your finance will go to savings.

5. **Investing:** This is a discussion about your risk tolerance, how best to invest in property, stocks, bonds, starting your own business or whether to do it at all.

6. **Retirement:** Finally, you'll want to talk about how to plan for your golden years.

What are the areas from the above list that need your attention?

1. _____ 2. _____ 3. _____

What happens in a lot of marriages is that only one person handles and understands the finances. That leaves the other person with little knowledge about the truth of the money. This set-up can get your marriage into a lot of trouble.

Both spouses need to be crystal clear about the details of your finances. Otherwise, the money can become the ultimate power struggle. Whenever there is a power struggle, someone wins and someone loses. Don't let this happen in your Happy Marriage.

On the next page is a Sample Budget. Most couples say they know their money well and are super clear about where it all goes. The results may surprise you.

Monthly Money In	Amount
Salary	$
Rental Income	$
Investment Dividends	$
Inheritance	$
Total:	**$**

Monthly Money Out	Amount
Mortgage	$
Real Estate Tax	$
Groceries	$
Credit Card	$
Electric	$
Cable	$
Cell Phone	$
Cash	$
Gas	$
Car Payment	$
Car Insurance	$
Car Tax	$
Garbage collection	$
Water	$
Private School Tuition	$
Club Payment	$
Fuel	$
Private Store Credit Cards $	$
Pet Expenses	$
House Cleaning	$
Child Care	$
Vacations	$
Miscellaneous	$
Total	**$**

If you cannot discuss money because it leads to fighting or you don't fully understand the budget, then Money Is Mastering YOU.

However if you take charge, communicate and decide together to get a handle on your finances, then YOU are Mastering Your Money. When you are both responsible together for mastering your money...it will enable your Happy Marriage to stay on track.

Remember to bring your finances to your Weekly Meeting so that you both are educated on where the money is and how it is spent. You should BOTH know and understand the finances even if only one of you manages it. This is a lifetime habit that will save you much marital distress. Remember to put the focus on how you can both prosper together.

"A budget is telling your money where to go instead
of worrying where it all went."

- Dave Ramsey

Lock In the Learning

What is one action you will take toward your marital finances?

_____

_____

_____

_____

NOTES

_____

_____

_____

_____

_____

_____

_____

_____

_____

_____

Remember To   _____

Share Your New   _____

Insights With   _____

Your Spouse   _____

_____

_____

Solution # 6

Encourage Intimacy, Sex & Celebration

Solution #6 for a Happy Marriage is to ensure you take time for intimacy, sex and celebration. When these areas are promoted, marriage can be a non-stop adventure where both spouses feel appreciated and loved.

What is the main problem for most marriages? Everyone is way too busy. The Office for National Statistics finds that on average married spouses spend 2.5 hours a day with the person they love...including weekends. That is not a lot of time.

And when couples are together, this is what they do:

- 1/3 of their time together is spent watching TV
- 1/4 of their time – eating
- 1/4 of their time – doing chores

Here are 3 Strategies for spending more meaningful time together.

1) Encourage More Intimacy
2) Have More Sex
3) Celebrate More Often

1) Encourage more Intimacy for a Happy Marriage

So how can you do create more intimacy in your Happy Marriage? An intimate relationship is an interpersonal relationship that involves physical or emotional intimacy. It is characterized by friendship, platonic love, romantic love and sensual activity.

Let's look at 4 Types of Intimacy that you should be engaged in for your Happy Marriage to succeed.

Intimacy comes in many shapes, including conversation, cuddling, a touch, an embrace, a glance, a massage. There are many ways to participate in shared moments.

- Intellectual intimacy is where two people exchange thoughts, share ideas and enjoy similarities and differences between their opinions.
- Experiential intimacy is where couples enjoy an experience together such as playing tennis or attending a concert.
- Emotional intimacy is where two persons can comfortably express their feelings with each other.
- Physical intimacy is any form of sensual expression with each other. It might be holding hands or lying close together in a hammock.

Let's Be Honest
(Write the answers below in the space provided)

How important is intimacy to your marriage?

_____

_____

_____

_____

Which of the previous types of intimacy is your marriage in need of the most?

_____

_____

_____

_____

When do you feel closest to your spouse?

_____

_____

_____

_____

Name the most intimate moment you have had with your spouse?

_____

_____

_____

_____

How could you create more moments of intimacy?

_____

_____

_____

_____

Tracy's Tip

If you want to have a lifetime of intimacy it needs to start with friendship and fun. If you are having trouble finding things to talk about then try a conversation starter game like "Table Topics" or other card games that initiate ideas for getting to know one and other on a more intimate level. Or you can decide to trade date nights. One Saturday, you plan the date and do something unexpected and the following Saturday have your spouse plan an evening out as well. If you keep things between you enjoyable and entertaining, your Happy Marriage will benefit in more ways than one.

2) Encourage More Sex For A Happy Marriage

Having sex is an extremely personal act. Couples can feel very vulnerable regarding sexual activity. Fear of rejection, not performing well enough, body insecurities or anxiety about disclosing an unusual sexual desire can stop you from communicating freely.

In fact, many people find it extremely difficult to talk about sex at all. Compounding the problem is the mistaken notion that sex is something you should be instinctively good at it, which just isn't true. In reality the key to becoming a good lover is to have good communication with your partner.

1. Most people find it very difficult to talk about sex
2. It is a myth that you should be naturally good at sex
3. Many people fear rejection from their partner
4. Many people fear not performing well
5. Most people have body issues
6. Most people have anxiety about discussing sex

Let's Be Honest
(Write the answers below in the space provided)

How would you rate or typify your sex life?

_____

_____

_____

_____

What's missing from your sex life for you?

_____

_____

_____

_____

What is your favorite part of your sex life?

_____

_____

_____

_____

What is the most troubling part of your sex life?

_____

_____

_____

_____

Do you have any fears about sex? If so, what?

_____

_____

_____

_____

What is your definition of great sex?

_____

_____

_____

_____

Are there any sexual fantasies you would like to experiment with?

_____

_____

_____

_____

How will you discuss the above answers with your spouse?

_____

_____

_____

_____

Would more open communication about sex in your marriage be beneficial?

_____

_____

_____

3) Encourage More Celebration For A Happy Marriage

People like to put an exclamation point on different events in their lives. It is a way of defining what they are most proud of and taking a moment to savor the blessings in their lives. There are at least five reasons it is critical to celebrate your Happy Marriage more than once a year.

1. It reaffirms your marriage
2. It demonstrates gratitude and support for your union
3. It gives you something to look forward to and excited about
4. It is a source of pride and accomplishment
5. It proclaims to the world the goodness of marriage

Name 3 new activities that would help celebrate your marriage?

1)_____

2)_____

3)_____

How do you think your spouse would like to celebrate your marriage?

_____

_____

_____

_____

What specifically will you do about scheduling some time to celebrate?

_____

_____

_____

_____

A Happy Marriage is where two best friends also enjoy passion and deep abiding love. Intimacy, sex and celebration are the first things to disappear in a troubled or harried marriage. Try some of the following ideas to keep all three strategies at the top of your Happy Marriage priority list:

- Turn off electronics when you are together
- Schedule a date night EVERY week
- Get away on vacation so you can concentrate solely on each other
- Play games and do activities that you both enjoy
- Listen to each other's physical needs and desires
- Have FUN!!!

"If I get married, I want to be very married."

- Audrey Hepburn

Lock In the Learning

What is one action you will take to create more intimacy in marriage?

_____

_____

_____

_____

NOTES

_____

_____

_____

_____

_____

_____

_____

_____

_____

_____

_____

_____

_____

_____

_____

Remember To   _____

Share Your New   _____

Insights With   _____

Your Spouse   _____

Solution # 7

Revere Conflict

Solution #7 for a Happy Marriage is to revere conflict in your marriage as a divine opportunity to be your best self. Marital struggle can be a mirror to your own soul and a welcome encounter for personal evolution. Can you imagine how different your marriage would be if you thought of every single problem as an opportunity to take the high road? Here we uncover the truth that marriage is always exposing areas of our own life (not our partner's) that needs to be improved. Marriage can be the greatest of all tools to encourage and confront questions of character, integrity, selflessness and generosity.

What many people do during conflict with their spouse is put the magnifying glass on the other person and find fault. Instead we must learn to revere conflict by making a decision to investigate how YOU could show up differently. Could you be more generous, more gentle, more forgiving, more kind, and more patient during the worst of times?

Let's Be Honest
(Write the answers below in the space provided)

The Question is...How are YOU showing up during conflict?

What is your fighting style?

_____Get mad but keep quiet

_____Withdraw to a safe spot and give silent treatment

_____Get angry and go on offensive

_____Give in and tell your spouse that they are right

_____Deny. Pretend you have no idea why your spouse is upset

_____Peace at any price

If you could improve your fighting style, what would you do differently?

_____

_____

_____

_____

In what subjects do you tend to have conflict with your spouse?

_____

_____

_____

_____

How did your parents fight? Do you want to fight differently?

_____

_____

_____

_____

Are you fighting in front of your kids?   YES____NO____

If so, what will you do about that?

_____

_____

_____

_____

If there was a mirror to your own soul, what lesson would you be forced to learn about yourself regarding conflict with your spouse?

_____

_____

_____

_____

How exactly will you show up differently during conflict to improve your marriage?

_____

_____

_____

_____

Tracy's Tip

Conflict and anger are often associated with one another but, in fact, they are not the same thing. Conflict involves a difference of opinion; and anger is an emotion that you can control. It is important to remember that you do not have to get angry about differences of opinion with your spouse. Instead you could embrace the idea that having a different opinion from your spouse is a gift because it expands the possibilities.

During conflict what other behavior could you choose instead of anger? (Gentleness, understanding, patience, love, forgiveness, agreeing to disagree, allowing my partner be right)

_____

_____

_____

_____

Here are some "Rules" of Marital Battle that I have outlined that will enable you to have a Happy Marriage even during conflict.

1. Do <u>NOT</u> fight in front of your children ever. It makes them feel afraid and insecure. Often kids think they caused the argument and it creates anxiety for them. This is true at ANY AGE. Don't deceive yourself into thinking they are too young to understand or pick up on distress. Go outside away from your children during arguments.

In what way do you need to improve in this area?

_____

_____

_____

_____

2. Do <u>NOT</u> threaten each other with divorce. Agree to never bring that word into any argument you are engaged in.

In what way do you need to improve in this area?

_____

_____

_____

_____

3. Do <u>NOT</u> attack the person, instead attack the problem.

In what way do you need to improve in this area?

_____

_____

_____

_____

4. Set Boundaries. Everyone deserves to be treated with respect, even during an argument. If your spouse yells at you, belittles you or calls you names, ask them to stop. If they continue, walk away.

In what way do you need to improve in this area?

_____

_____

_____

_____

5. Find the Real Issue. Most arguments happen when a spouse's needs are not being met. Try to look beneath the immediate details and get to the heart of the matter. It is really not about who left the toothpaste top off the toothpaste.

In what way do you need to improve in this area?

_____

_____

_____

_____

6. Let the other person be right once and a while. This might be hard for some of you, but decide to choose peace over your ego or vanity.

In what way do you need to improve in this area?

_____

_____

_____

_____

7. When you can't find common ground. Agree to disagree. Figure out what you can agree on. Decide to validate what the other person is saying and be curious about why they have a different point of view. Resolve your differences before bedtime and do not go to sleep mad.

In what way do you need to improve in this area?

_____

_____

_____

_____

Tracy's Tip

Every time there is a marital disagree ask this question instead:

How can we BOTH win???

This is my favorite question and it leads to a much more positive solution during disagreements. Since the question usually predicates the answer, decide to ask better questions. It is amazing the answers you will come up with if you take this approach and bring it into all your marital disagreements.

Revering conflict has several benefits

1. It enables you to keep the focus on yourself as you grow and learn about being the best YOU

2. It teaches you to fight fair and with a generous heart

3. It reminds your family that you can disagree and still love and cherish one and other

4. It sets you up to have a Happy Marriage for a lifetime

5. It encourages you to investigate and be curious about why your spouse has a different opinion. The world would be a very boring place if we all experienced everything the exact same way. Learn to enjoy your differences.

Following are some strategies to employ during conflict in marriage.

Test yourself to see where you could improve.

Negotiate When Possible: Get in the habit of "negotiating" conflict. Let's say your spouse wants to go camping and you want to stay at a 5-star hotel. Negotiate a deal where you spend two nights in the tent and two nights in a luxury suite.

Do you need to work on this area? YES____NO____

Consider That You Love This Person: Remind yourself that an argument does not have to change how the two of you feel about each other.

 Do you need to work on this area? YES____NO____

Be Curious: Look at your spouse's point of view as a gift. It is a blessing to have another opinion completely different from yours. Be curious and have some fun with where you both see things differently.

Do you need to work on this area? YES____NO____

Use a Mirror: Stop pointing the finger in blame and ask yourself if you are showing up as the best and most honorable person you can be. Are you pleased with your choices and conduct?

Do you need to work on this area? YES____NO____

Be Forgiving: A happy home starts and ends with forgiveness.

Do you need to work on this area? YES____NO____

Based on the answers above, what do you need to work on?

1)_____

_____

_____

_____

2)_____

_____

_____

_____

3)_____

_____

_____

_____

4)_____

_____

_____

_____

"Success in marriage does not come merely through finding the right mate, but through being the right mate."

\- Barnett Brickner

Lock In the Learning

What is one action you will take to revere conflict?

_____

_____

_____

_____

NOTES

_____

_____

_____

_____

_____

_____

_____

_____

_____

_____

_____

_____

_____

_____

Remember To   _____

Share Your New   _____

Insights With   _____

Your Spouse   _____

                  _____

Solution # 8

Go Team Parent

Solution #8 for a Happy Marriage is to proclaim "Go Team Parent" as your motto. Allow house rules, schedules, and parenting styles to unite you instead of divide you. You both want to raise healthy, happy kids, so create a home full of peace and mutual respect. Solid parenting begins with both spouses agreeing on rules and demonstrating a team approach to how your family will interact.

"Go Team Parent" means that you and your spouse get super clear on all the tasks necessary to create a happy home and then you go work together to get the job done. Every child is unique and every family deals with issues differently at all the stages and ages of a child's life. Decide ahead of time that you and your spouse will be on the same page and find common ground.

Positive parenting hinges on BOTH you and your spouse upholding the rules and expressing them in love. This is what GO TEAM PARENT is all about.

I have coached in many homes and the one thing that creates the most chaos for kids and their parents is not having consistency or clarity around how the family home operates.

For the best results agree to agree on parenting strategies. Once they are established, never contradict each other in front of your children, never play "good cop, bad cop" and never have your children get different answers depending on which parent they ask. Instead simply GO TEAM PARENT.

Do Rules:

All good rules should be specific and easy to understand. There are 'do' rules that are best in most situations because they guide your child's behavior in a positive way. Examples are:

- Sit down to eat
- Speak in a polite voice
- Wear your seatbelt in the car
- Be home by curfew

Don't Rules:

You can also have 'don't' rules that you use less frequently. Examples are:

- Don't spit
- Don't use profanity
- Don't text and drive

Tracy's Tip

Just remember that kids model a parent's behavior. If you tell your kids not to text and drive and then they see you text and drive...they most likely will end up texting and driving.

What Can Parents Do To Enforce Rules

1. Parents can agree on which rules to set

2. Parents can post the rules so everyone can know them

3. Parents can ask all caregivers to monitor these rules

4. Parents can remind children in a regular family meeting

What grade do you give yourself in terms of great parenting?

A_____ B_____ C_____ D_____

How could you do better in regard to great parenting?

_____

_____

_____

_____

Let's Be Honest
(Write down your answers in the space provided)

What family rules do you and your spouse agree on?

1)_____

_____

_____

2)_____

_____

_____

3)_____

_____

_____

What family rules do you not agree on, but can negotiate?

1._____

2._____

3._____

What will you do to make sure everyone agrees on family rules?

_____

_____

_____

_____

Great Parenting Suggestions

1. Turn off your cell phone and give full attention to your kids

How could you do better in this area?

_____

_____

_____

_____

2. Make bedtime a precious & consistent ritual

How could you do better in this area?

_____

_____

_____

_____

3. Show physical affection every day. Lots of smiles and hugs

How could you do better in this area?

_____

_____

_____

_____

4. Spend quality time with each child individually

How could you do better in this area?

_____

_____

_____

_____

5. Discipline your children ONLY with love and affection

How could you do better in this area?

_____

_____

_____

_____

6. Be a great role model

How could you do better in this area?

_____

_____

_____

_____

7. Involve children in decision-making. Get them to buy-in

How could I do better in this area?

_____

_____

_____

_____

8. Play with your kids because kids just want to have fun

How could you do better in this area?

_____

_____

_____

_____

9. Encourage, guide and teach. Never ridicule, yell or belittle

How could you do better in this area?

_____

_____

_____

_____

Tracy's Tip

Never Shame Your Children. Shame has long-term effects on children and can set them up for a lifetime of low self-esteem and struggle. You can condemn the child's behavior without condemning the child. Agree To Love Your Children For Who They Are ... Not Who You Want Them To Be. This is one of the biggest mistakes I see in parenting. Just love and enjoy your kids for who they are!!!

There is a great quote which says,
 "Go and love someone exactly as they are. And then watch how quickly they transform into the greatest, truest version of themselves. When one feels seen and appreciated in their own essence, one is instantly empowered." - Wes Angelozzi

Best Parenting Ideas of All Time

I tell all my coaching clients that the best way to parent is by encouraging from the bottom up, not scolding from the top down. Kids want to feel included in the team approach to a Happy Family dynamic. The following tips may help you!

- Get Your Kids To Buy-In. Invite your children to a weekly family meeting. Discuss what works and what all of you can do differently to support a Happy Home.

- Mirror back what your children are saying so they feel understood. If a child seems frustrated or angry, you can respond, "What I hear you saying is that you are very upset and angry." This immediately settles them, as they feel heard and acknowledged.

- Speak to your kids sitting or standing side-by-side instead of in direct confrontation. If you want good communication, take them for a ride in the car, out to a counter for lunch, or an activity like walking, where you line up shoulder to shoulder which indicates you're on the same side.

- Apologize to your kids if you have done something wrong. Have them understand you are also capable of mistakes and capable of being sorry for those mistakes.

- Tell your kids EVERY DAY how proud you are of them. Build them up into the people you want them to be. It works every time.

- Reading to your children at bedtime or praying over them is one of the best things you can do to share a moment together.

- Finally....There is NOTHING better for family harmony than the family dinner table. There is an overwhelming number of studies that link family dinners to a lowering of all high risk behaviors for kids. From school problems, smoking, binge drinking to even depression and suicidal thoughts. Family dinners promote positive interactions that ultimately contribute to both home life and society at large. Family dinners create a sense of identity, security and love for children. Family dinners also provide such a magical degree of belonging that researchers say it is has a more positive effect on kids than even good grades or church attendance. Make sure you are having dinner with your children at least 4 times a week. Don't let busy schedules run your family life. Take control and do what is best for you and your children.

In 20 years from now when someone asks your child to tell them about his/her parents...(That's YOU)...What is it that you hope they will say?

_____

_____

_____

_____

Whatever your answer is..start working on it now.

"What is it like to be a parent? It is one of the hardest things you will ever do, but in exchange it will teach you the meaning of unconditional love."

- Nicholas Sparks

Lock In the Learning

What is one action you will take toward "Go Team Parent"?

_____

_____

_____

_____

NOTES

_Remember To
Share Your New
Insights With
Your Spouse_

Solution # 9

Forgive, Forget, Get A Fresh Start

Solution #9 for a Happy Marriage is to treasure forgiveness as the key to a happy union. Forgiveness is not a one-time act but a continual way of being toward one and other. You agree on mercy and pardon as good policy in your partnership. Forgive, forget and get a fresh start.

A nationwide Gallup poll found that 94% of people said it was important to forgive. Studies show that individuals who are not able to forgive are still thinking about the ramifications five years later. As C. S. Lewis said, "Everyone says forgiveness is a lovely idea until they have something to forgive."

Forgiveness is a subject that comes up quite a bit in marriage. Offenses are common; both big and small. Usually the offender wants to be forgiven but the offended can be reluctant to forgive as there is perceived power in holding onto the hurt. Often spouses become grudge holders. This is an extremely unhealthy stance to take in marriage.

Forgiveness is not just about saying the words "I forgive you." It is an active, ongoing process in which you make a conscious decision to let go of negative feelings whether the other person deserves it or not. (Let's read that AGAIN)

How To Forgive

1. You recognize that you are, first and foremost, in need of forgiveness. Recognizing your own shortcomings is key because it helps you understand that everyone is capable of mistakes and ultimately deserves forgiveness.

2. Make a decision to offer that forgiveness to your spouse.

3. Understand that forgiveness does not let your spouse off the hook for bad behavior, but is a starting point toward positive change.

4. Depend on God to give you the strength needed to forgive. For many couples forgiving a betrayal seems impossible.

5. Pray for your spouse if they have hurt you. Remember that God loves your spouse more than you do and wants them to grow in enlightenment. By praying for your spouse, you are "letting Go and letting God."

6. Reconcile with humility. Agree to reconnect no matter who is right or who is wrong. Make it your marital policy to not spend more than 24 hours with an unforgiving heart. As Mother Teresa said: "To forgive takes love, But to forget takes humility."

7. Offer forgiveness to your spouse. Accept forgiveness from your spouse. Make this an ongoing ritual.

Tracy's Tip

Recover Quickly

I am going to use a sports analogy to make this next point.

What do Serena Williams, Lionel Messi, and Lebron James have in common?? What makes them champions in their sport of choice? It is not just natural talent, it is also hard work and ability to recover quickly from a bad shot; a tennis shot, a soccer shot or a basketball shot. All of these athletes attribute their success to a quick recovery. When something goes wrong, they don't keep mulling it over and over again, instead they decide to recover immediately and get back into the game. It makes them winners! And you can do the same thing in married life. Learning to recover quickly from offenses can set you up for a lifetime of Happy Marriage.

Let's Be Honest
(Write down your answers in the space provided)

What are your feelings about forgiveness in marriage?

_____

_____

_____

_____

What do you need to be forgiven for in this marriage?

_____

_____

_____

_____

What offense do you need to forgive your spouse for?

_____

_____

_____

_____

How could you learn to extend forgiveness more easily?

_____

_____

_____

_____

Can you go to your spouse and offer/accept forgiveness?

_____

_____

_____

_____

If you both forgave each other, how would that make you feel?

_____

_____

_____

_____

Is there anything you need to forgive yourself for?

_____

_____

_____

_____

Remember forgiveness equals vulnerability. The great thing about being married....or should be...is that you can be completely yourself, including all your good qualities and all your bad qualities...and still be deeply loved. Decide to make your Happy Marriage a soft place to fall. A place where you know the other person has your best interest at heart and you have theirs at heart too. This requires vulnerability. Vulnernability is not a liability. Vulnerability is where you discover your truest and most authentic humanity.

Benefits of Forgiveness

- You enjoy healthier relationships
- Less anxiety, stress and conflict
- Fewer symptoms of depression
- Higher self esteem
- Greater spiritual and psychological well being
- You Will Be Happier!!!

"A Happy Marriage is the union of two forgivers."

\- St. Simeon

Lock In the Learning

What is one action you will take regarding forgiveness?

_____

_____

_____

_____

NOTES

_____

_____

_____

_____

_____

_____

_____

_____

_____

_____

_____

_____

_____

_____

Remember To _____

Share Your New _____

Insights With _____

Your Spouse _____

Solution # 10

Keep The Faith

Solution #10 for a Happy Marriage is to explore ways to maintain and strengthen your faith. It is critical to examine what spiritual practices are important to you individually; and to your family as a whole. There is fifty years of research suggesting that spouses praying together and worshiping together has a magical degree of positive power over family health. Couples were significantly happier and experienced far fewer problems with anxiety, depression, and substance abuse when they had a foundation of faith in their marriage.

It turns out that 80% of Americans get married in a religious ceremony.

Most people want God in the <u>GETTING</u> married.

However, too often people forget God In the <u>STAYING</u> married.

In this chapter, you are going to examine your own faith practices as well as whether you consider your marriage a contract or a sacred covenant.

Let's Be Honest
(Write down your answers in the space provided)

Who is God for you?

_____

_____

_____

_____

What code of ethics guides your life?

_____

_____

_____

_____

What kind of prayer is comfortable and satisfying to you?

_____

_____

_____

_____

How important is it that your spouse shares your religious beliefs?

_____

_____

_____

_____

Would you like your spouse to support your spiritual rituals?

_____

_____

_____

_____

How would you like to promote more faith in your marriage?

_____

_____

_____

_____

Spiritual Practices

The best way to promote faith is through spiritual practices. A spiritual practice is the regular performance of activities undertaken for the purpose of cultivating spiritual development. It is really just getting to know and experience God at a deeper level.

Let's Look At 5 Practices for A Happy Marriage.

#1 Spiritual Practice - Power of Prayer For A Happy Marriage

The Divorce Rate in America is at a minimum of 1 in 2 marriages end in divorce. Statistics suggest that for those that pray together, the divorce rate is 1 in 10,000. That is remarkable.

It turns out those couples that prayer together, stay together.

What is Prayer?

Prayer is primarily a conversation with God. It is the interaction of the human mind, heart, and soul with God, not only in contemplation or meditation, but also in direct address to Him. Prayer may be oral or mental, occasional or constant, formal or informal.

The very act of praying is an implicit recognition of the presence of God. To be sincere in our prayer, we must have faith that we can actually communicate with God. Moreover, we must also believe that God is interested in communicating back with us.

If you find a regular time to pray and a regular place to pray such as a church pew, the beach, or your favorite room of your home – you are much more likely to pray.

Tracy's Tip

Here are some simple suggestions regarding prayer in marriage:

1. **Commit to praying together at a regular time**
2. **Find a special place that would trigger you to pray**
3. **Invite the whole family to pray at mealtime or bedtime**
4. **Share a prayer from your childhood**
5. **Spend two minutes listening for God's reply after you pray**

What new habit would help you promote prayer in your marriage?

_____

_____

_____

_____

What is one thing you will do differently in your marriage regarding prayer?

_____

_____

_____

_____

2 Spiritual Practice - Power of Worship For A Happy Marriage

Attending a church service can supply more than just a weekly routine. It is place to be reminded of morality, fidelity, devotion and forgiveness. Moreover, friendships get established that lend support to couples facing the ordinary joys and challenges of married life. Plus, children gain significant knowledge about God in respective church curriculums.

Do you think weekly worship would benefit marriage/family life?

_____

_____

_____

_____

Do you and your spouse agree on weekly worship as important?

_____

_____

_____

_____

Which of the following would you hope to promote in your Happy Marriage?

Worship Promotes:	Choose One or More
Sexual Fidelity	
Morality	
Forgiveness	
Family-friendly social networks	
Religious Education For Children	
Support During Trials and Tragedy	

Tracy's Tip

There are many more distractions on weekends than there used to be, which makes getting to a religious service on Saturday or Sunday almost impossible. Sports commitments, shopping and time off all seem to be taking first place. If you want to get to a house of worship, you must make it a top priority.

What is one thing you will do differently in your marriage regarding worship?

_____

_____

_____

_____

#3 Spiritual Practice - The Power of Gratitude For A Happy Marriage

Start and end your day in gratitude for each other, for God, for all of your blessings. There are innumerable benefits associated with gratitude including better health, deeper happiness, more sleep, stronger relationships and an overall sense of well-being.

What you focus on expands into every nook and cranny of your life, so focus on the good stuff for your Happy Marriage.

Tracy's Tip

Start your day in gratitude, keep a gratitude journal, and encourage everyone in your home to share what they are grateful for at the family dinner table.

What is one thing you will do differently in your marriage regarding gratitude?

_____

_____

_____

_____

#4 Spiritual Practice - The Power of Stillness For A Happy Marriage

Stillness is the absence of motion, noise and distraction toward a moment of harmony with God. Being still is increasingly more challenging as we live in a time where we are always plugged in and constantly on the go. To know God, you must be still.

Tracy's Tip

Turn off electronics regularly and get in the habit of listening for God.

What is one thing you will do differently in your marriage regarding stillness?

_____

_____

_____

_____

#5 Spiritual Practice – The Power of Fasting

Another great spiritual practice is fasting. Most people understand fasting as abstaining from food as you hunger for a deeper relationship with God. However there are many other things you can fast from in an attempt to keep the focus on God and honor His presence in your life.

You could fast from:

- Gossip
- Hatred
- The Need To Be Right
- Defensiveness
- Criticizing Others
- Selfishness
- An Unforgiving Heart

Try one of these and watch miracles happen!

Is there some bad habit you would be willing to fast from for the benefit of your Happy Marriage?

_____

_____

_____

_____

What is one thing you will do differently in your marriage regarding fasting?

_____

_____

_____

_____

Finally,

Do You Believe Your Marriage is a Contract or a Covenant or Both?

There are two types of marriage. One is a contract and one is a covenant. It is often the difference between a marriage and Holy Matrimony.

A contractual marriage is a contract between husband and wife, to their respective rights and obligations in regards to the marriage.

A covenant marriage is intended by God to be a lifelong relationship exemplifying unconditional love, reconciliation, sexual purity, and growth. It is a commitment with God that you will honor each other and have God be the centerpiece of your partnership.

YIKES…You mean there are three of us in this marriage?

In a Covenant Marriage – God is fully present.

Do you view your marriage as a contract, a covenant, or both?

_____

_____

_____

_____

Contract: I take you for myself.
Covenant: I give myself to you.

Contract: You had better do it!
Covenant: What can I do for you?

Contract: What do I get?
Covenant: What can I give?

Contract: I'll meet you halfway.
Covenant: I'll give you 100% plus.

Contract: I have to.
Covenant: I want to.

If you thought of your marriage as a covenant, how would you behave differently?

_____

_____

_____

_____

What do you think God is calling you to do in your marriage?

_____

_____

_____

_____

"God created marriage. No government subcommittee envisioned it. No social organization developed it. Marriage was conceived and born in the mind of God."

- Max Lucado

Lock In the Learning

What is one action you will take toward keeping the faith?

_____

_____

_____

_____

NOTES

Remember To
Share Your New
Insights With
Your Spouse

Marriage

If you want something to last forever,
you treat it differently.

~

You shield it, and protect it.
You never abuse it.

~

You don't expose it to the elements,
you don't make it common or ordinary.

~

If it ever becomes tarnished, you lovingly
polish it until it gleams like new.

~

It becomes special because you have
made it so, and it grows more beautiful
and precious as time goes by.

- Burton Howard

Lock In the Learning Checklist

At the end of each chapter you were invited to lock in the learning by committing to one new action step for each solution mentioned in this book. Write them again here and go create the Happy Marriage of Your Dreams!!!

1)_____

_____

_____

2)_____

_____

_____

3)_____

_____

_____

4)_____

_____

_____

5)_____

_____

_____

6)_____

_____

_____

7)_____

_____

_____

8)_____

_____

_____

9)_____

_____

_____

10)_____

_____

_____

About the Author

Tracy Fox is a sought after speaker, best-selling author and strategic life coach. Tracy works with clients in two specific areas. One is Personal Life Coaching where she consults with men and women who are unhappy, stuck, and don't know what to do about it. Her second area of expertise is in Marriage Coaching where she teaches couples how to reclaim the joy of married life.

Tracy is also the author of the highly popular, *Having A Heart For God Devotional, 365 Days of the One Minute Bible Study* which has received a 5-star rating on Amazon. She also sends out a free, weekly, inspirational email entitled, *"Empower Yourself"* to thousands of readers.

Tracy has recently created a 10 week video E-Course, "Happy Marriage – A 10 Step Solution to Happily Ever After" which is available at her website. www.TracyFox.net

Tracy is married to Mark Fox, and they live in Darien CT with their three sons, and dog, Finnegan.

To Order More Copies Of
Happy Marriage Handbook

Or

To Request
Tracy Fox Signature Life or Marriage Coaching
In Person Or Via Telephone

Or

To Subscribe to The Happy Marriage E-Course

* * *

Email Tracy at: Tracy@TracyFox.net

Call: 203 856-2906

Visit Our Website: www.TracyFox.net

I look forward to hearing from you!

TRACY FOX

Speaker – Author – Life Coach

Made in the USA
Middletown, DE
23 April 2024

53316194R00068